JAN 15

# THE GHOSTS OF CIVIL WAR SOLDIERS

John Perritano

PowerKiDS press

New York

Published in 2015 by The Rosen Publishing Group, Inc.
29 East 21st Street, New York, NY 10010

First Edition

Editor: Joanne Randolph
Book Design: Contentra Technologies
Illustrations: Contentra Technologies

## Publisher's Cataloging Data

Perritano, John.
The ghosts of Civil War soldiers / by John Perritano — first edition.
p. cm. — (Jr. graphic ghost stories)
Includes index.
ISBN 978-1-4777-7133-4 (library binding) — ISBN 978-1-4777-7134-1 (pbk.) — ISBN 978-1-4777-7135-8 (6-pack)
1. Ghosts—United States—Juvenile literature.  2. United States—History—Civil War, 1861–1865—Miscellanea—Juvenile literature. I.  Perritano, John. II. Title.
BF1472.U6 P47 2015
398—d23

Manufactured in the United States of America

CPSIA Compliance Information: Batch #WS14PK2: For Further Information contact Rosen Publishing, New York, New York at 1-800-237-9932

# Contents

# Introduction

When Abraham Lincoln was elected president in 1860, the issue of slavery was heavy on his mind. Slave owners in Southern states worried that Lincoln would try to outlaw slavery, taking away a major source of labor for many landowners. To save their way of life, Southern states chose to **secede** from the United States. Lincoln declared that states could not simply leave, and with the hope of preserving the Union, the Civil War began. It was a brutal war, resulting in hundreds of thousands of lives lost. According to some, not all of those who died are truly gone, though. Legends tell of unexplained sights and sounds experienced by many who visit the places where lives were lost in this terrible war.

# Main Characters

**John Brown** (1800–1859) A man of action, Brown was determined to stop the spread of slavery and to free the slaves. In 1855, he moved to the Kansas Territory. There, he and his sons killed five proslavery settlers. He then set his sights on arming the slaves and staging a **revolt**.

**Robert E. Lee** (1807–1870) Lee was a loyal and highly respected US soldier. When the Civil War began, President Abraham Lincoln asked Lee to take command of Union forces. Lee declined and resigned from the army when Virginia seceded.

**Abraham Lincoln** (1809–1865) The sixteenth president of the United States, Lincoln was a firm believer that the country could not be made of both free and slave-holding states. Lincoln believed the Southern states could not legally form their own nation and called up troops to force those states back into the Union. By 1863, Lincoln shifted the war's focus by **emancipating** the enslaved people.

# The Ghosts of Civil War Soldiers

THE US CIVIL WAR BEGAN ON APRIL 12, 1861. THAT'S WHEN CONFEDERATE SOLDIERS ATTACKED FORT SUMTER, A US ARMY OUTPOST LOCATED IN CHARLESTON HARBOR, SOUTH CAROLINA.

THE WAR SPLIT THE UNITED STATES. ON ONE SIDE WAS THE UNION. ON THE OTHER WAS THE CONFEDERACY.

Union

Confederacy

FT. SUMTER

OH, MAMA. HELP ME! HELP ME, MAMA!

HUSH UP, YOU CHOSE TO FIGHT FOR THE CONFEDERACY. NO ONE CAN HELP YOU NOW. MAY YOUR **TRAITOROUS** SOUL BURN FOR **ETERNITY**!

"THE WAR **RAGED** FOR FOUR BLOODY YEARS, AS UNION SOLDIERS FROM THE NORTH TRIED TO KEEP THE COUNTRY TOGETHER AND END SLAVERY IN THE SOUTH."

"THE CIVIL WAR ENDED IN APRIL 1865 WITH A UNION VICTORY. MORE THAN 600,000 AMERICANS DIED DURING THE FIGHTING."

"PEOPLE SAY THAT SOME SOLDIERS NEVER LEFT THE BATTLEFIELD. THEY STILL HAUNT THE PLACES WHERE THEY PERISHED."

# John Brown's Ghost

TWO YEARS BEFORE THE WAR BEGAN, JOHN BROWN, AN **ABOLITIONIST**, TRIED TO START A SLAVE REVOLT IN HARPERS FERRY, VIRGINIA.

BROWN AND HIS GROUP STORMED THE FEDERAL **ARSENAL** TO STEAL GUNS. THEY WANTED TO ARM THE SLAVES.

MAKE HASTE, LADS! THE LORD WILL PROTECT US AND DELIVER THE SLAVE FROM HIS BRUTAL MASTER.

KEEP WORKING. YOUR DAY IS NOT DONE YET!

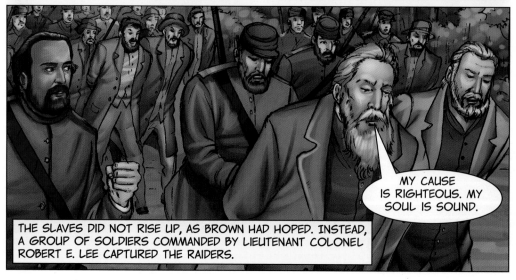

MY CAUSE IS RIGHTEOUS. MY SOUL IS SOUND.

THE SLAVES DID NOT RISE UP, AS BROWN HAD HOPED. INSTEAD, A GROUP OF SOLDIERS COMMANDED BY LIEUTENANT COLONEL ROBERT E. LEE CAPTURED THE RAIDERS.

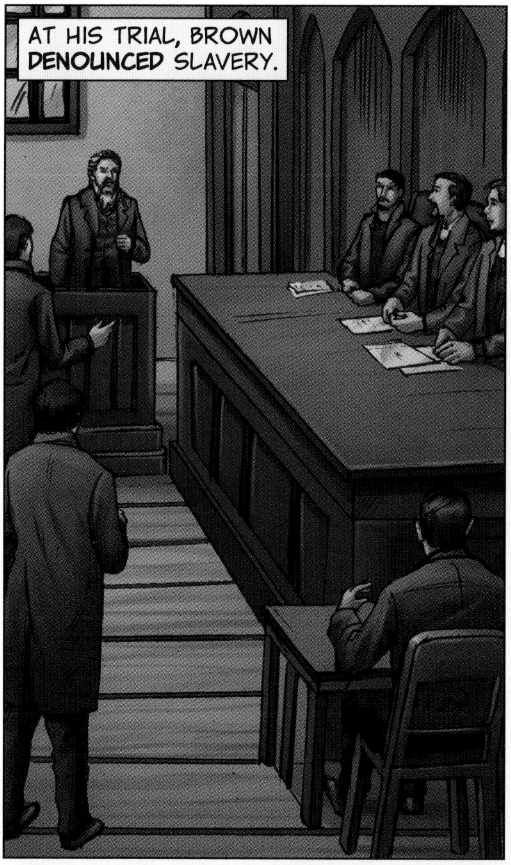
AT HIS TRIAL, BROWN **DENOUNCED** SLAVERY.

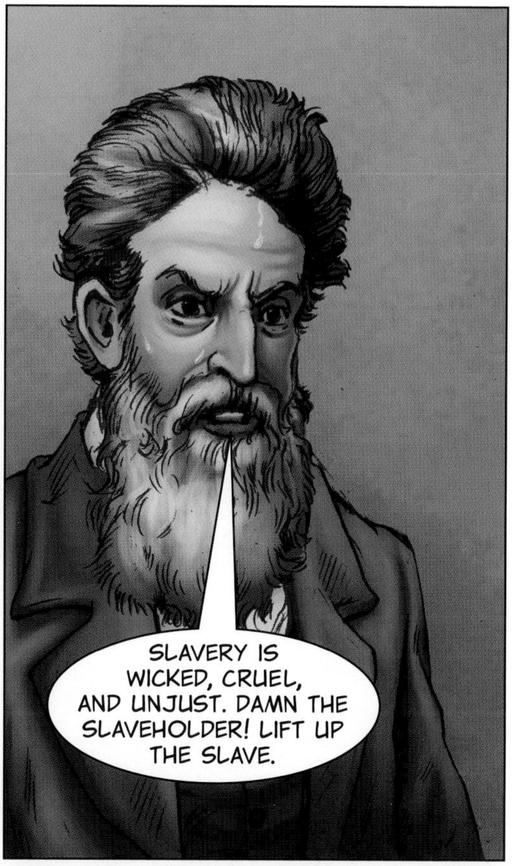
SLAVERY IS WICKED, CRUEL, AND UNJUST. DAMN THE SLAVEHOLDER! LIFT UP THE SLAVE.

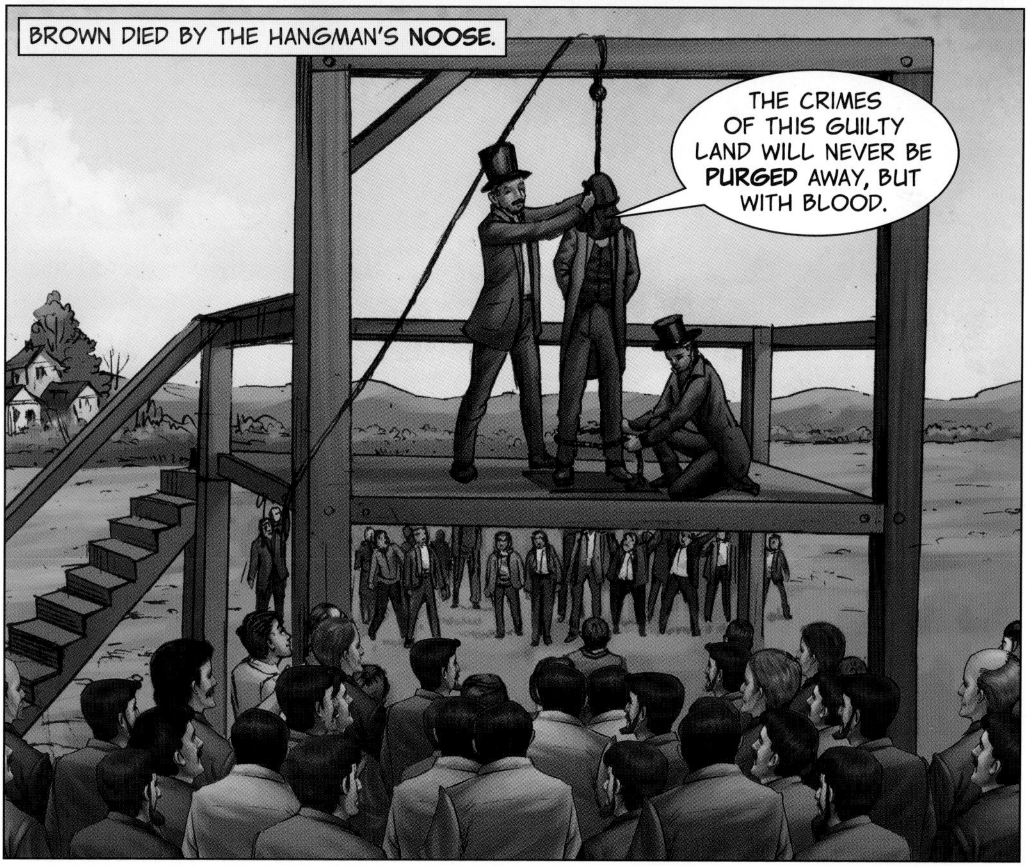
BROWN DIED BY THE HANGMAN'S **NOOSE**.
THE CRIMES OF THIS GUILTY LAND WILL NEVER BE **PURGED** AWAY, BUT WITH BLOOD.

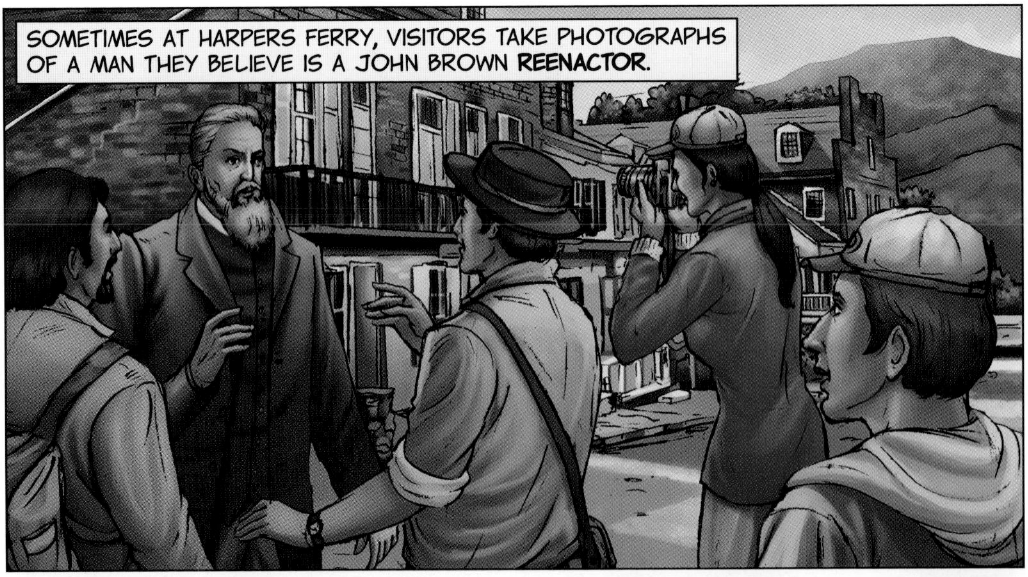
SOMETIMES AT HARPERS FERRY, VISITORS TAKE PHOTOGRAPHS OF A MAN THEY BELIEVE IS A JOHN BROWN **REENACTOR**.

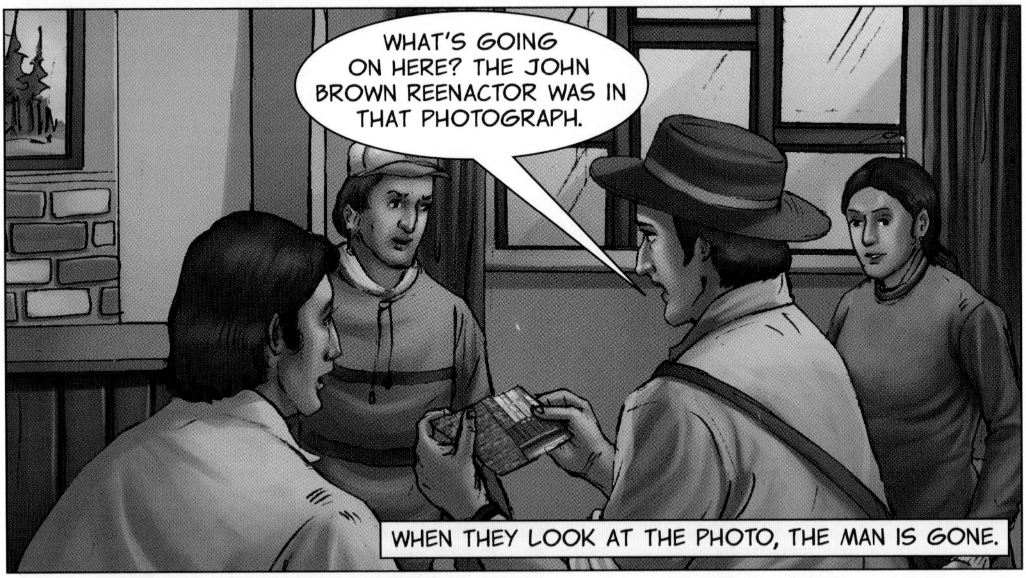
WHAT'S GOING ON HERE? THE JOHN BROWN REENACTOR WAS IN THAT PHOTOGRAPH.
WHEN THEY LOOK AT THE PHOTO, THE MAN IS GONE.

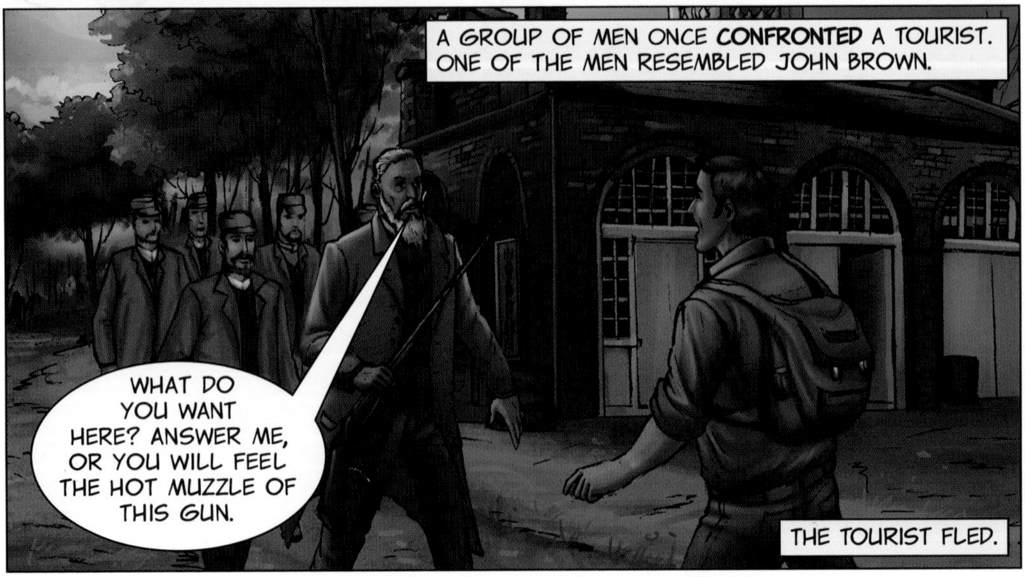
A GROUP OF MEN ONCE **CONFRONTED** A TOURIST. ONE OF THE MEN RESEMBLED JOHN BROWN.
WHAT DO YOU WANT HERE? ANSWER ME, OR YOU WILL FEEL THE HOT MUZZLE OF THIS GUN.
THE TOURIST FLED.

# Shiloh's Phantom Drummer Boy

WHEN WAR CAME, MANY BOYS VOLUNTEERED FOR THE UNION AND CONFEDERATE ARMIES. THEY WERE TOO YOUNG TO SIGN UP LEGALLY, BUT AS LONG AS THEY LOOKED OLD ENOUGH, THEY WERE **MUSTERED** INTO THE RANKS.

ARE YOU SURE YOU'RE OLD ENOUGH, LAD?

SURE, SERGEANT. WE ALL ARE.

YOUNG BOYS OFTEN SERVED AS DRUMMERS. THEIR DRUMS COULD BE HEARD ABOVE THE NOISE OF THE BATTLE, AND THEY PROVIDED INSTRUCTIONS TO THE TROOPS.

IN APRIL 1862, YANKEE SOLDIERS FACED THE **REBELS** AT A CHURCH IN TENNESSEE CALLED SHILOH.

NO, BOY, NOT "ATTACK." SOUND "RETREAT!" SOUND "RETREAT!"

I NEVER LEARNED "RETREAT," SIR!

UNION TROOPS ATTACKED THE REBEL POSITIONS AS A YOUNG DRUMMER BEAT THE CALL TO ATTACK.

SPURRED ON BY THE DRUMMER BOY'S BEAT, THE YANKEES OVERRAN THE CONFEDERATES.

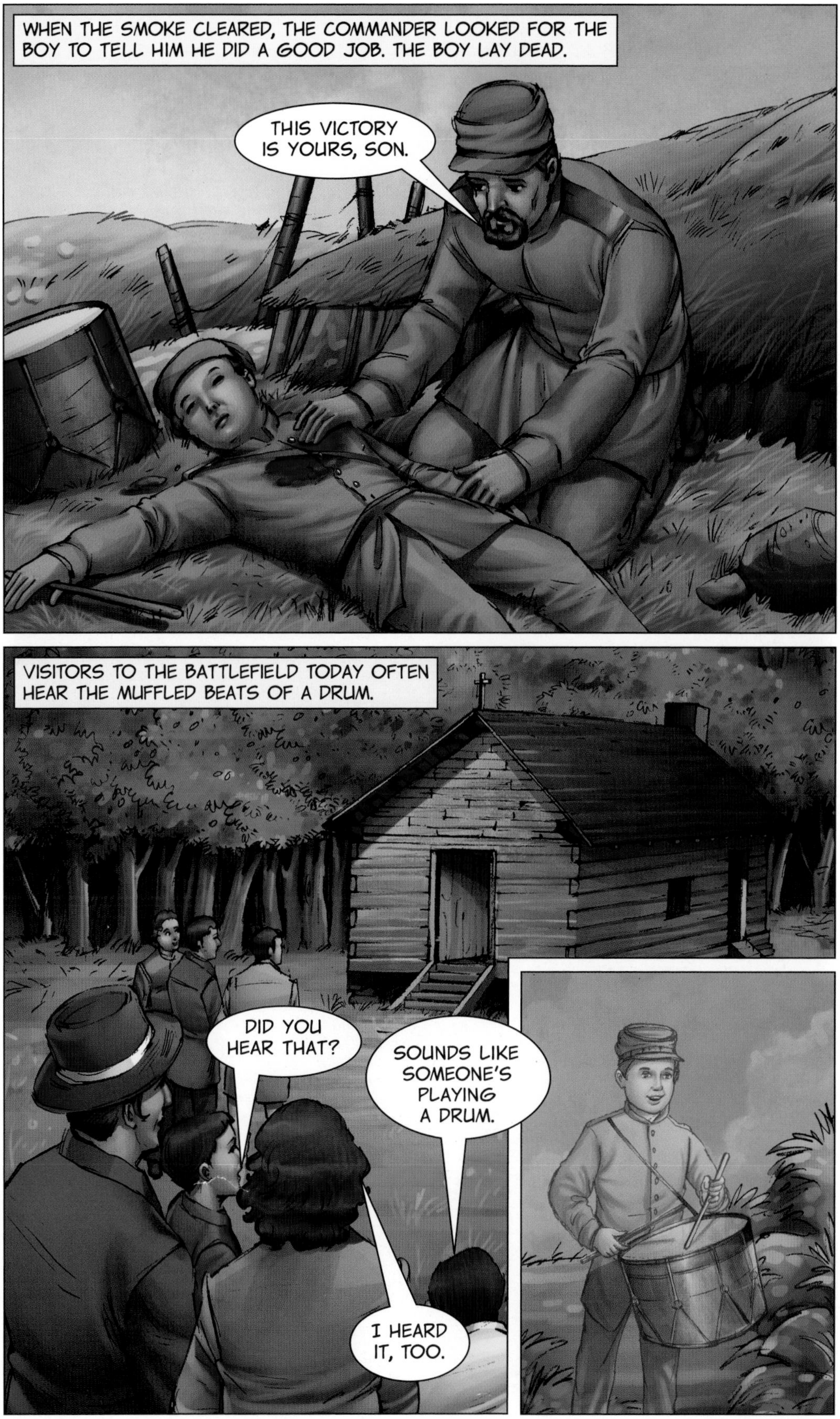
WHEN THE SMOKE CLEARED, THE COMMANDER LOOKED FOR THE BOY TO TELL HIM HE DID A GOOD JOB. THE BOY LAY DEAD.
THIS VICTORY IS YOURS, SON.
VISITORS TO THE BATTLEFIELD TODAY OFTEN HEAR THE MUFFLED BEATS OF A DRUM.
DID YOU HEAR THAT?
SOUNDS LIKE SOMEONE'S PLAYING A DRUM.
I HEARD IT, TOO.

VISITORS TO THE SHILOH BATTLEFIELD ALSO HEAR THE SOUNDS OF BATTLE AS THE PHANTOM DRUMMER BOYS DUTIFULLY CALL OUT THE SIGNAL TO ATTACK.

# The Ghosts of Bloody Lane

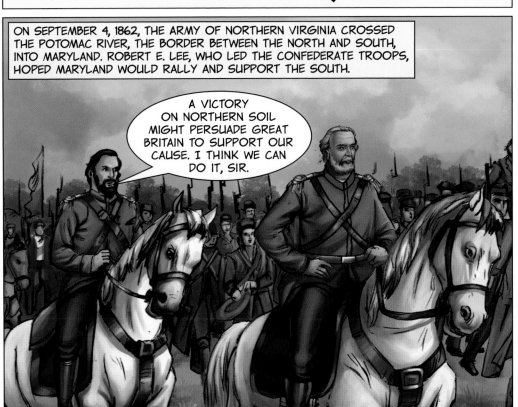

ON SEPTEMBER 4, 1862, THE ARMY OF NORTHERN VIRGINIA CROSSED THE POTOMAC RIVER, THE BORDER BETWEEN THE NORTH AND SOUTH, INTO MARYLAND. ROBERT E. LEE, WHO LED THE CONFEDERATE TROOPS, HOPED MARYLAND WOULD RALLY AND SUPPORT THE SOUTH.

A VICTORY ON NORTHERN SOIL MIGHT PERSUADE GREAT BRITAIN TO SUPPORT OUR CAUSE. I THINK WE CAN DO IT, SIR.

ON SEPTEMBER 17, LEE'S TROOPS BATTLED UNION FORCES NEAR ANTIETAM CREEK JUST OUTSIDE SHARPSBURG, MARYLAND. IT WOULD BE THE BLOODIEST DAY IN AMERICAN HISTORY.

BY MIDMORNING, FIGHTING HAD SHIFTED TO A SUNKEN ROAD RUNNING THROUGH A CORNFIELD. IT WAS A GOOD PLACE FOR THE CONFEDERATES TO HIDE.

KEEP FIRING, BOYS. KILL THOSE YANKEES.

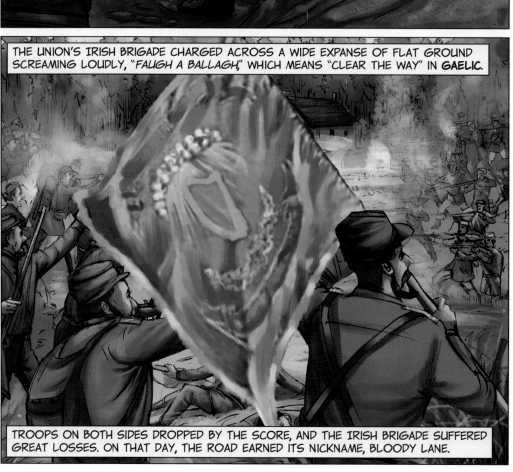

THE UNION'S IRISH BRIGADE CHARGED ACROSS A WIDE EXPANSE OF FLAT GROUND SCREAMING LOUDLY, "FAUGH A BALLAGH," WHICH MEANS "CLEAR THE WAY" IN **GAELIC**.

TROOPS ON BOTH SIDES DROPPED BY THE SCORE, AND THE IRISH BRIGADE SUFFERED GREAT LOSSES. ON THAT DAY, THE ROAD EARNED ITS NICKNAME, BLOODY LANE.

OVER 100 YEARS LATER, A GROUP OF SEVENTH GRADERS VISITED BLOODY LANE.

DO YOU HEAR THAT?

SOUNDS LIKE SOME MEN ARE YELLING.

DON'T BE SILLY. WE'RE THE ONLY ONES HERE.

THAT WAS A GREAT TRIP, BUT NOW WE HAVE TO WRITE AN ESSAY ABOUT WHAT WE SAW.

NOT JUST WHAT WE SAW. I'M WRITING ABOUT WHAT I HEARD, TOO.

THIS IS VERY STRANGE. MOST OF THESE CHILDREN SAY THEY HEARD A CHRISTMAS CAROL SUNG IN A FOREIGN LANGUAGE DURING OUR FIELD TRIP. I THOUGHT I HEARD IT, TOO.

15

THE TEACHER KNEW ABOUT THE GAELIC WAR CRY, BUT HE NEVER TOLD HIS CLASS. WHEN YELLED, "FAUGH A BALLAGH" SOUNDS SIMILAR TO "FA-LA-LA-LAH," THE GHOSTLY CHRISTMAS CAROL THE STUDENTS HEARD.

# The Horseman of Little Round Top

IN JUNE 1863, GENERAL LEE INVADED THE NORTH AGAIN, PUSHING INTO PENNSYLVANIA.

ON JULY 1, 1863, THE CONFEDERATES INCHED CLOSER TO GETTYSBURG. UNION **CAVALRY** SPOTTED THEM. AFTER A DAY-LONG BATTLE, THE CONFEDERATES CHASED THE OUTNUMBERED UNION TROOPS THROUGH GETTYSBURG.

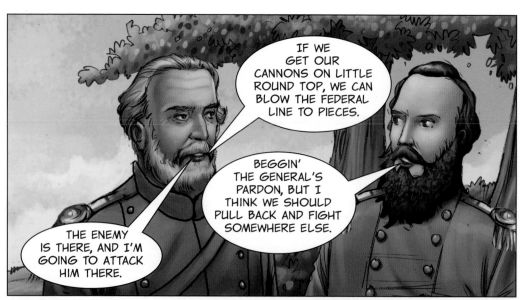

IF WE GET OUR CANNONS ON LITTLE ROUND TOP, WE CAN BLOW THE FEDERAL LINE TO PIECES.

BEGGIN' THE GENERAL'S PARDON, BUT I THINK WE SHOULD PULL BACK AND FIGHT SOMEWHERE ELSE.

THE ENEMY IS THERE, AND I'M GOING TO ATTACK HIM THERE.

ON JULY 2, THE CONFEDERATE TROOPS SCRAMBLED UP LITTLE ROUND TOP. THEY ALMOST BROKE THE UNION LINE ON THE HILL . . .

. . . UNTIL JOSHUA CHAMBERLAIN AND HIS GROUP OF UNION TROOPS BEAT BACK THE CONFEDERATE ASSAULT.

SOMETHING ELSE HAPPENED THAT DAY. SOLDIERS SAY THEY SAW AN **APPARITION** OF AN OFFICER ON HORSEBACK URGING THE UNION SOLDIERS ON. NO ONE KNEW WHERE HE HAD COME FROM, BUT HE WAS SOON GONE, LIKE A MIST ON THE WIND.

THEN, UNION FORCES WON THE BATTLE.

# Lincoln's Ghost

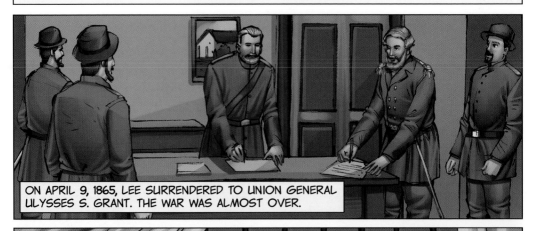

ON APRIL 9, 1865, LEE SURRENDERED TO UNION GENERAL ULYSSES S. GRANT. THE WAR WAS ALMOST OVER.

ON APRIL 14, PRESIDENT LINCOLN WENT TO THE THEATER WITH HIS WIFE. AS LINCOLN WATCHED THE PLAY *OUR AMERICAN COUSIN*, JOHN WILKES BOOTH SHOT THE PRESIDENT, FATALLY WOUNDING HIM.

THE PRESIDENT DIED THE NEXT DAY, ON APRIL 15, AT A HOUSE ACROSS THE STREET FROM THE THEATER.

IT IS SAID THAT THE GHOST OF ABRAHAM LINCOLN STILL HAUNTS THE WHITE HOUSE, OFTEN APPEARING AT TIMES OF NATIONAL CRISIS.

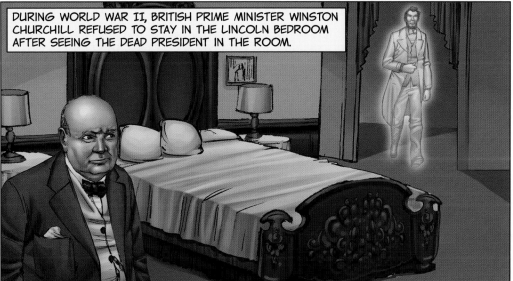

DURING WORLD WAR II, BRITISH PRIME MINISTER WINSTON CHURCHILL REFUSED TO STAY IN THE LINCOLN BEDROOM AFTER SEEING THE DEAD PRESIDENT IN THE ROOM.

MANY MEN GAVE THEIR LIVES FIGHTING FOR WHAT THEY BELIEVED IN. WE MAY NEVER BE ABLE TO EXPLAIN THE SIGHTS AND SOUNDS THAT MANY CLAIM COME FROM GHOSTS, BUT THE MEMORY OF THE WAR THAT COST SO MANY LIVES WILL STAY WITH OUR COUNTRY FOREVER.

# More on Civil War Ghosts

- **National Soldier's Orphan Homestead**
  An old orphanage built after the Civil War in Gettysburg is said to be haunted by the children of Union soldiers who died during the war. At the time, the National Soldier's Orphan Homestead was home to 130 boys and girls. By all accounts, it was a pleasant place to live until a brutal woman named Rosa Carmichael became headmistress. She constantly beat the children and chained them to the basement walls. She also forced many to crawl into a basement "dungeon," where they **languished** until they learned whatever lesson Carmichael wanted to teach them. If you tour the house today, you can crawl inside the dungeon and hold on to one of the wire chains that once held the tiny arms of orphans. It is said that people can still hear the cries and screams of the tortured children.

- **The Farnsworth House**
  The Farnsworth House on Baltimore Street, in Gettysburg, sheltered Confederate sharpshooters who took aim at the Union lines on Cemetery Hill during the Battle of Gettysburg. Dozens of rebel soldiers crawled into the basement. Today, workers and visitors to the Farnsworth House claim to see and experience a variety of ghosts, including the spirit of a young boy who was hit and killed by a runaway horse and buggy.

- **Eliza Thompson House**
  The Eliza Thompson House, in Savannah, Georgia, is said to be haunted by a rebel soldier killed by a horse in front of the property. At the time, the house was occupied by Eliza and Joseph Thompson and their seven children. Today it is an inn, and in room 132, guests have heard the laughter of children during the night. Some people have been pushed out of bed. As for the Confederate soldier who died on the property, many people have seen his face looking out the window of the room.

# Glossary

**abolitionist** (a-buh-LIH-shun-ist) A man or woman who worked to end slavery.

**apparition** (a-puh-RIH-shun) A ghost or something ghostly.

**arsenal** (AHR-sih-nul) A storehouse of weapons.

**cavalry** (KA-vul-ree) The part of an army that rides and fights on horseback.

**confronted** (kun-FRUNT-ed) Challenged someone face-to-face.

**denounced** (dih-NOWNSD) Spoke out against, often publicly.

**emancipating** (ih-MAN-sih-payt-ing) Freeing from the restraint, control, or power of another, usually referring to the freeing of slaves.

**eternity** (ih-TUR-nuh-tee) Forever.

**Gaelic** (GAY-lik) The Celtic languages of Ireland and Scotland. Irish Gaelic is usually called Irish.

**languished** (LANG-gwishd) Suffered neglect or became weak.

**mustered** (MUHS-terd) Brought together, or assembled a group of soldiers.

**noose** (NOOS) A loop at the end of a rope with a knot through which the loop can be tightened.

**purged** (PURGD) Got rid of something.

**raged** (RAYJD) Happened or continued in a violent or intense way.

**rebels** (REH-bulz) People who fought for the South during the Civil War.

**reenactor** (ree-eh-NAK-tur) A person who pretends to be a person from another time.

**revolt** (rih-VOHLT) A fight against an authority.

**secede** (sih-SEED) To withdraw from a group or a country.

**traitorous** (TRAY-tur-us) Guilty of betraying one's country or showing disloyalty.

# Index

# Websites

Due to the changing nature of Internet links, PowerKids Press has
developed an online list of websites related to the subject of this book.
This site is updated regularly. Please use this link to access the list:

www.powerkidslinks.com/jggs/civil/